A B C

animal alphabet

by

Laerta Premto

Copyright © 2023 Laerta Premto
ISBN 979-8-9878808-0-7
All rights reserved.

laertapremto.com

Dedicated to my nephews, Noah and Theo.

Alpacas come in 22 colors and hundreds of shades.

Alpaca

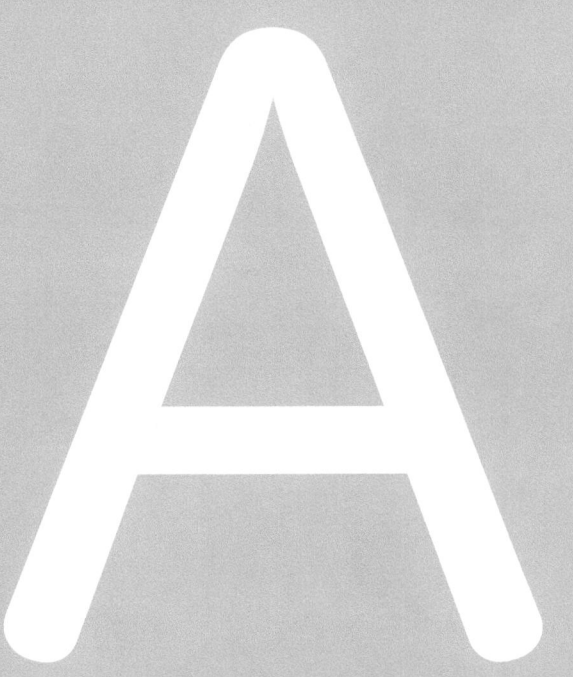

Bears use scent to communicate messages over long distances.

Bear

Cows can smell you from 6-miles away.

Cow

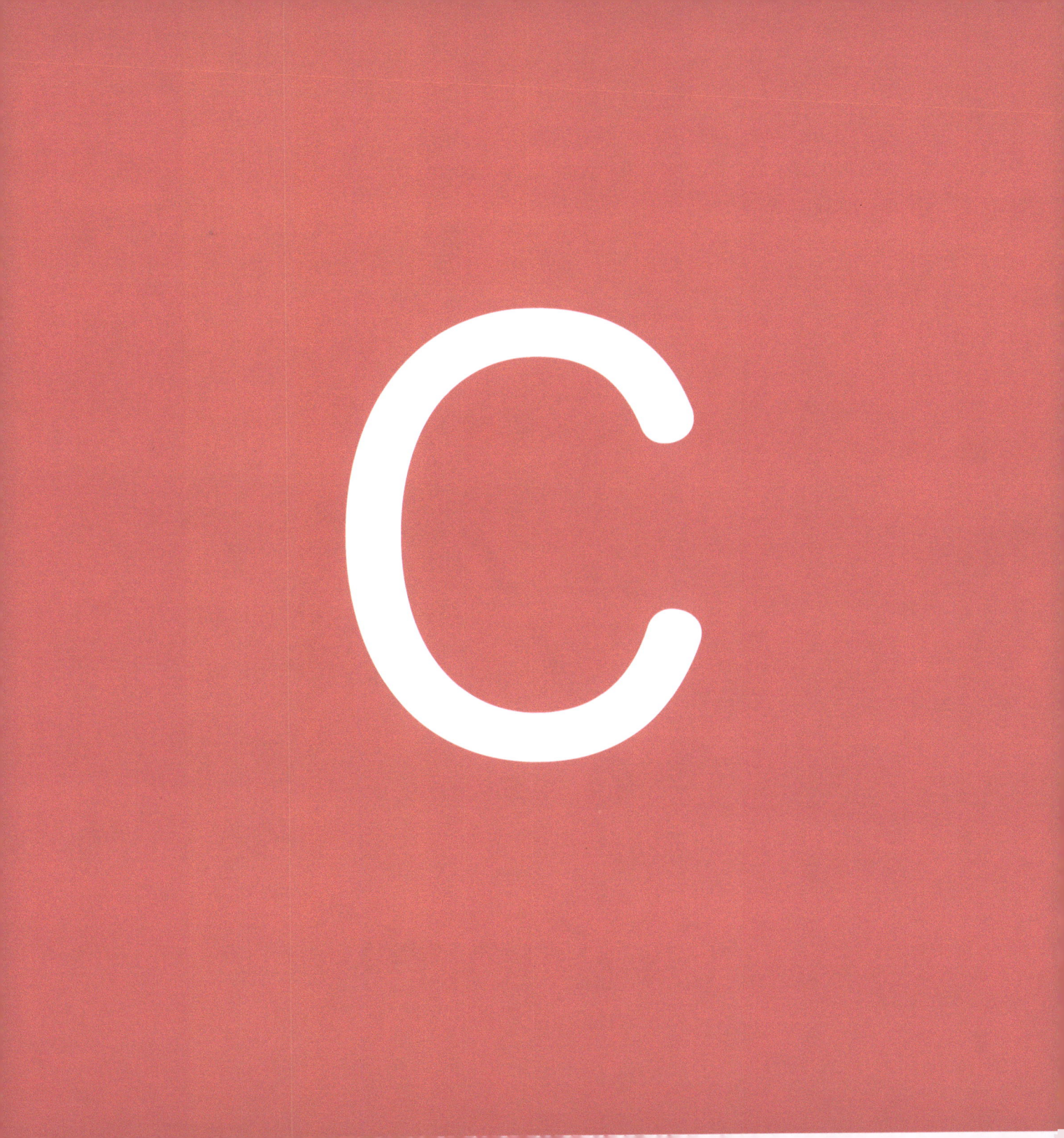

Dragonflies have two sets of wings so they can fly straight up or down, go backwards, fly upside down and hover.

Dragonfly

Elephants can use their trunks to smell, trumpet, drink and grab things.

Elephant

E

Flamingos can sleep standing on one leg.

Flamingo

Giraffes are the tallest mammals on Earth with females growing to 14 ft tall and males towering at 18 ft tall.

Giraffe

G

Hippos produce their own sunblock!

Hippo

H

Impalas can leap up to 10 feet in the air.

Impala

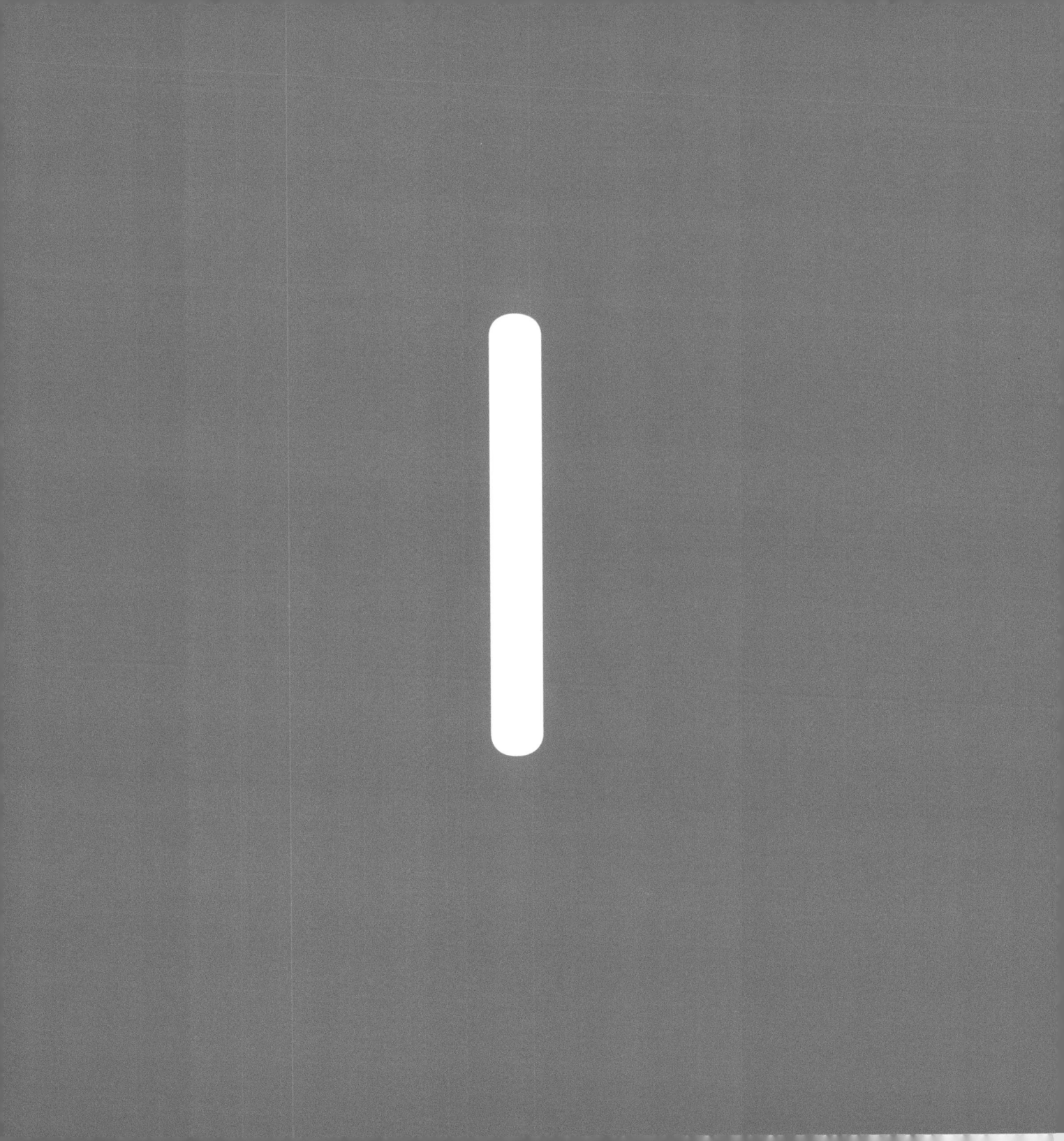

Jellyfish don't have a heart, lungs or a brain either!

Jellyfish

Kangaroos use their tails as a fifth leg.

Kangaroo

Lions are the only cats that roar together.

Lion

Monkeys live both on the ground and in the trees.

Monkey

M

Narwhal tusks are actually teeth, which can grow up to 10 feet.

Narwhal

N

Octopuses have three hearts: two just to pump blood through the gills and one more to circulate it to the organs.

Octopus

Many male **penguins** gift female penguins with rocks in order to woo them.

Penguin

P

Quail live in flocks during the winter so they can gather together for warmth.

Quail

Rabbits communicate using a secret code.

Rabbit

R

Snails can sleep for up to 3 years especially when temperatures get really dry.

Snail

S

India is the country with the largest number of wild **tigers**.

Tiger

Sea Urchins can live up to
200 years in the wild.

Sea Urchin

Vipers are a group of poisonous snakes that have sharp fangs.

Viper

Whales have a long life span ranging from 20 years to 100 years.

Whale

W

X-Ray fish are known for their translucent skin that allows their organs and skeleton to be observed, much like an X-Ray.

X-Ray Fish

Yaks can tolerate temperatures of up to -40 degree Fahrenheit.

Yak

Zebras are herbivores, which means they eat plants, grasses, and roots.

Zebra

z

Let's practice!

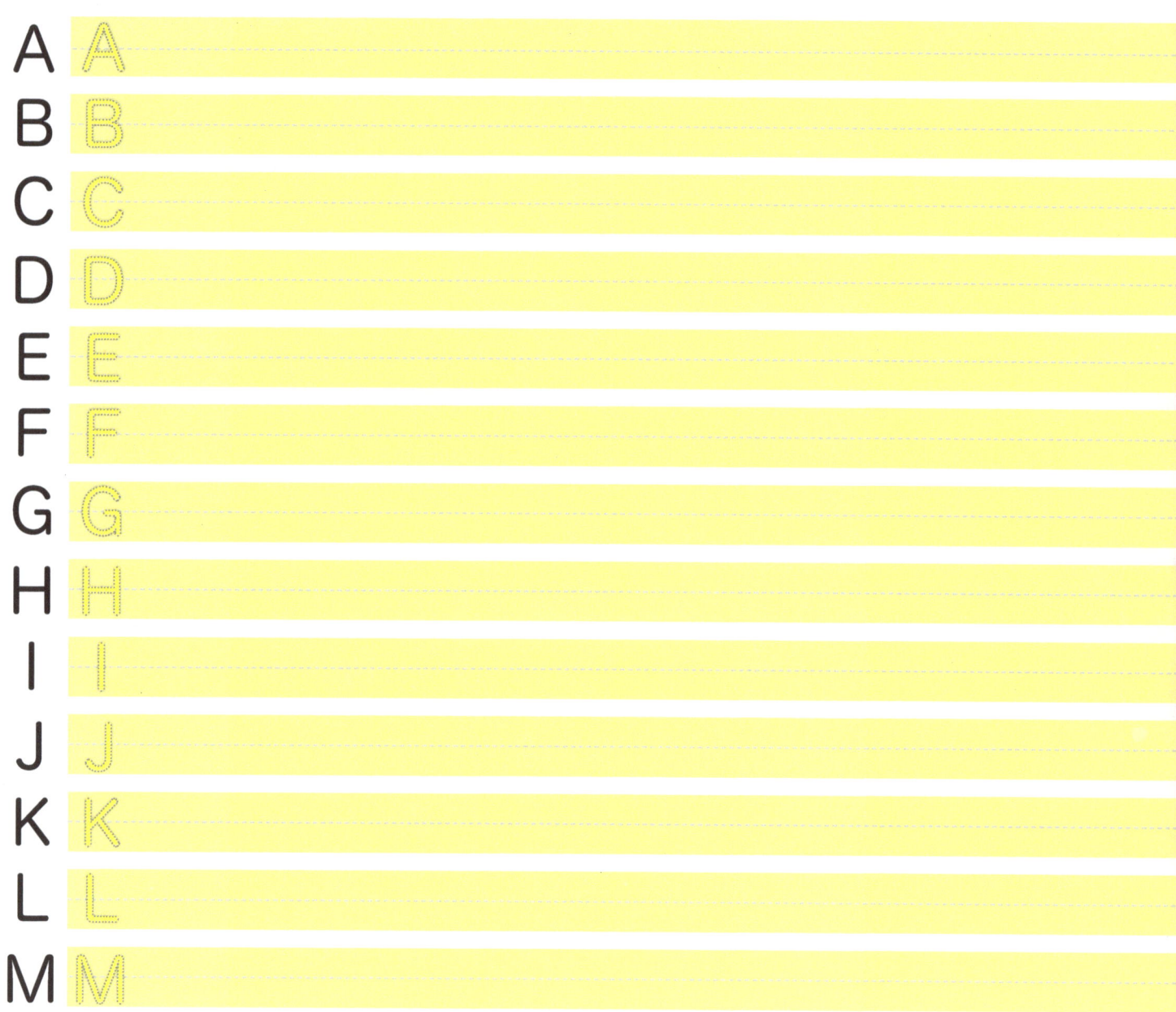

Grab a pen or pencil and practice writing each letter below.

N N
O O
P P
Q Q
R R
S S
T T
U U
V V
W W
X X
Y Y
Z Z

Laerta Premto is an artist, designer and world traveler who inspires others to learn and grow through her whimsical illustrations.

Follow Laerta's adventures and upcoming artwork on Instagram @laertapremto.

Laerta painted the illustrations for this book in Ecuador, and designed the book in France before completing it in the US.

> Learning is a treasure that will follow its owner everywhere.

Chinese Proverb

Laerta Premto

laertapremto.com

www.ingramcontent.com/pod-product-compliance
Lightning Source LLC
Chambersburg PA
CBHW061358090426
42743CB00002B/59